Time Management For Lawyers

How to Double Your Free Time

By Mike Young, Esq.

Dedication

To my son, Peyton, who made this book possible by providing every incentive to spend time being a good parent in addition to practicing law.

Copyright Notice

For more information, please read the ***Disclosures and Disclaimers*** section at the end of this Book.

First Edition, June 2012

Published by Business Performance Advisors LLC (the "Publisher").

Rules of Professional Conduct

Because this book discusses ways you can save time in your law practice, it's possible that something said may conflict with your state bar rules.

If there is a conflict, you'll obviously want to obey applicable bar rules. Please let me know about the particular conflict and I'll add it to the *Recommended Resources* section at http://TimeManagementLawyers.com as an update for this book.

Although this book is designed to at least double your free time, the caveat is that competent representation of your clients takes priority. That being said, if you apply the strategies and tactics, you will free up time plus do a better job representing your clients efficiently and effectively.

Continuing Legal Education

Some state bars allow self-study continuing legal education (CLE) credit. Check with the state bar(s) where you are admitted to practice law to see if your time spent reading this book qualifies for self-study CLE credit.

If your bar representative needs to see a copy of this book to determine whether you're eligible for credit, just email me the details at mike@timemanagementlawyers.com and a complimentary review copy of this book will be shipped to your state bar's CLE representative for evaluation.

Recommended Resources

To help you implement the time-saving strategies and tactics found within this book, I have set up a special *Recommended Resources* section for you that will be updated from time to time. For free access, just go to http://TimeManagementLawyers.com.

If you have suggested additions for the next edition of this book, please email them to me at mike@timemanagementlawyers.com.

Table of Contents

Introduction

Like other service professions, when you practice law, you're trading your time in exchange for money.

Why is this important?

Regardless of your current financial situation, time is your most valuable possession.

You can replace money. After all, it's just pieces of paper with numbers and portraits of dead presidents. If money is in short supply, the U.S. Federal Reserve simply prints more of it.

On the other hand, there are 168 hours in your week. The hours you invest in your practice cannot be replaced.

The purpose of this book is to at least double your free time. What you do with that time is up to you.

- If you're a workaholic, chances are you'll use this opportunity to expand your practice.
- If you want to spend time on personal activities instead of practicing law, this book will help you do that too.
- You may decide to take a "moderate" path by splitting your new free time between your law practice and your personal life.

It's your values and priorities that are at stake. If you allocate your time based upon other people's priorities or expectations for you, you're living their life instead of your own.

Instead, let's reclaim your time so you can spend it the way you want.

How to Use This Book

This book contains no-fluff practical advice on how to practice law so you can have a lot more free time to spend how you want to.

- If you're looking for motivational stories and positive affirmations designed to fill you with warm fuzzies about practicing law, this is not the book for you.

- If you're expecting a 500-page treatise filled with dry legalese or Socratic Method hide-the-ball nonsense, you will be disappointed.

- And if you're a Grammar Nazi, please suppress the urge to let me know the countless ways I've butchered the Queen's English.

You will get the best results if you read from the beginning to the end, highlight or bookmark the parts you want to implement, and then go back and put together a concrete plan to manage your time using the strategies and tactics you've learned.

On the other hand, if you're really pressed for time, start by reviewing the *Table of Contents*, pick a topic that interests you, read the chapter, and then implement the *Action Checklist* at the end of that chapter. For your convenience, there is a section to take notes at the end of each chapter in the print edition of this book.

Once you've read the entire book, at the end there's a *Master Action Checklist* for easy reference. This master checklist contains a review of all the Action Checklists for each chapter.

Chapter One: Goals

Why are you practicing law in the first place?

Does your law firm serve you or do you serve your practice?

In addition to representing your clients on weekdays, do you practice law on nights, weekends, and holidays too?

One of the main reasons why attorneys have time management issues is that there are no guiding goals to steer them in the right direction. If you don't know what you want, it's difficult to set priorities and spend your time accordingly.

So where do you start? Although there is overlap, set goals for your *professional* and *personal* lives.

Write the goals down and keep them in a place where you can refer to them several times a day. At a minimum, you'll want to review your goals as you begin the day and at night before you fall asleep to see how well you stayed on track with activities that were consistent with your goals.

Remember to keep the big picture in mind. Otherwise, your goals will be running contrary to your personal values.

For example, if you want to sell your law practice and retire at age 55, you'll need to do a lot more rainmaking now than if you plan to never retire but instead practice until the day you kick the bucket at age 95. The time commitment for each of these scenarios is very different.

If you want to become a stay-at-home parent within the next couple of years, it probably doesn't make much sense to set a conflicting goal of working 16-hour days to make partner at a sweatshop law firm you'll be leaving soon.

Action Checklist

1. Identify what you want to do with the rest of your life, including when or whether you plan to retire from practicing law.

2. Write down 3 professional and 3 personal goals consistent with your life plans.

3. Review these goals before you start work each day and in the evening to determine whether your personal and professional activities were consistent with your goals.

For more time management tools, tips and book updates, be sure to check out the *Recommended Resources* section at http://TimeManagementLawyers.com.

Your Notes: _____

_____

_____

_____

_____

_____

_____

_____

_____

_____

_____

_____

_____

_____

_____

_____

_____

_____

Chapter Two: The 80/20 Rule

Do you try to treat all of your clients equally? What about other things you work on daily in your law practice? How do you treat administrative tasks, rainmaking, and dozens of other firm-related activities you do every week?

When you treat all activities equal, this ignores the reality that each task generates unequal rewards for your efforts.

The 80/20 Rule[1] is a shorthand way of saying that your activities will create unequal results even if you invest the same of amount of time and effort into each.

It's also very likely 20% or less of your firm's clients will generate at least 80% of your revenues. The numbers will vary but 50% of your clients will not generate 50% of your income. In other words, the rewards for providing legal representation are not equal per client.

---

[1] The 80/20 Rule is sometimes referred as the Pareto Principle.

As an example, let's assume that 18% of your clients produce 85% of your revenue. The flip side of this is that 82% of your clients produce 15% of your revenue.

Does it make sense to treat all clients equally under these circumstances?

Of course not.

As long as you're competently representing all clients, there's absolutely no reason to focus on the 82% of your clients who produce only 15% of your revenue.

Instead, you want to devote your time to the vital few, those 18% who generate 85% of your firm's revenue.

To free up time to provide greater service to the profitable 18% of your client base, and to have a personal life, you should seriously consider getting rid of some or all of the 82% who bring so little to the table. You can do this by referral to another firm or bringing in a salaried associate attorney if the net income justifies it.

What about other parts of your law practice?

From a business standpoint, the highest and best uses of your time are (1) representing clients and (2) rainmaking to clone your best clients. These are your "vital few" activities, that is, the 20 part of the 80/20 Rule.

Yet you will find yourself doing many other activities during the day that are trivial because these actions deliver little or no reward for the time and energy you invest in them.

Delegate, outsource or dump the trivial many in order to focus on the few high value actions you can and should be taking as a legal professional.

Action Checklist

1. Identify the vital few clients who produce the majority of your income. Create a marketing plan for cloning them.

2. Identify the trivial many clients who suck up your time but add little to the bottom line. Create a plan for getting rid of them.

3. Make a list of tasks that you do unrelated to rainmaking or practicing law. Dump the unnecessary and delegate the rest.

For more time management tools, tips and book updates, be sure to check out the *Recommended Resources* section at http://TimeManagementLawyers.com.

Your Notes: _____

_____

_____

_____

_____

_____

_____

_____

_____

_____

_____

_____

_____

_____

_____

_____

_____

_____

Chapter Three: Templates

Are your written communications customized for that personal touch? Do you look for new ways to say the same thing in your letters, emails, legal documents etc?

Do you believe the effort to show yourself as individual pays off in the relationships that you build? Yet practicing law is designed for producing results for the client rather than fulfilling the creative desires of aspiring authors.

Every law office has tasks that can be partially or completely automated using written templates.

These include:

- Engagement, non-representation, collection, and routine cover letters.
- Email responses to common questions
- Signature lines on all written communications, including any boilerplate disclaimers
- Marketing materials, such as cards sent to existing clients
- Contract boilerplate (jurisdiction, alternative dispute resolution, etc.)
- Pleadings, motions, and discovery requests

If you find yourself writing the same thing repeatedly, it's time to create a template that can be used instead of starting from scratch each time.

You can also use text expanding software to insert template sentences and paragraphs in your documents and emails. These text expanders let you create a short-code by typing a few keystrokes that will populate your document with a template tied to that series of keystrokes.[2]

Note that if you're billing for your time, using templates will decrease the amount of work you do.

However, you can flat fee bill clients in many instances and make more in the process.

For example, let's say that a template enables you to prepare a simple motion in 30 minutes instead of 60 minutes it would take without the template. If you flat fee bill the client for preparing the motion, you can charge more than 30 minutes of billable time plus do other billable work in the free time created by using the template in the first place.

---

[2] The *Recommended Resources* section for this book at http://*TimeManagementLawyers*.com has links to text expanding software you may want to consider using.

What's key here is that you're disassociating value from the time you spend doing the work and focusing instead on the value of what you're delivering on the client's behalf. Templates enable you to make this change.

Action Checklist

1. Identify documents and email communications that you use repeatedly in your law practice.

2. Create templates and store them in a place accessible to you and others who will use them in your office. Where helpful, use text expanding software with these templates.

3. Set flat fee billing rates that fully compensate you for the value of the work done with each template instead so that you're getting paid for what you produce rather than the time it takes to produce it.

For more time management tools, tips and book updates, be sure to check out the *Recommended Resources* section at http://TimeManagementLawyers.com.

Your Notes: _____

_____

_____

_____

_____

_____

_____

_____

_____

_____

_____

_____

_____

_____

_____

_____

_____

_____

_____

Chapter Four: Parkinson's Law

Rather than get burned by failing to meet a court or client deadline, do you build in plenty of buffer time so that you can deliver?

If you believe that drafting a document is going to take two hours, do you pad it out by an extra hour or two so that you don't feel rushed.

It doesn't matter how much time you add as a buffer for completing a client matter. Chances are, you're rushing to get the work done, and wondering if you underestimated the time for completion.

To be fair, if you've practiced an area of law for at least a couple of years, you're probably a good judge of how much time something is going to take. The real reason you're rushing to complete the work is known as "Parkinson's Law."

Per this law, your work as a legal professional on any task will invariably expand to fill the time available for you to complete it. The excuse commonly given for wasting time is that you're engaged in zealous/competent representation of your client's interests. The extra time ensures you've done things right.

There are a few time frames that are beyond your control, such as the new client who walks in the door with a statute of limitations expiring that day.

However, in most cases, you choose how much time you're allotting for representing a client in a particular matter and your activities fill up that time even if you could have done the work in half the time. If you set 90 minutes for completing something, you'll likely take the full 90 minutes to do it. And odds are you could complete the same work in 70 or 80 minutes without the quality of your legal representation being adversely affected.

Why does this occur?

For two reasons.

First, when you've got extra time to do something for a client, you start focusing on trivialities rather than accepting you've done the heavy lifting and it's time to move on to the next legal matter.

Second, many attorneys are trained to be adrenaline junkies who procrastinate on doing work until there is a hard deadline for completing the work. Feeling rushed, they overestimate at the last minute what it is going to take to do the work right.

How many times have you pulled an all-nighter to deliver for a client? Looking back, you will discover in most instances you had plenty of daylight hours to complete the work if you hadn't procrastinated. The hours it should have taken you objectively would have been much less than your all-nighter.

So how do you get Parkinson's Law to work in your favor?

As much as practical, separate how you're paid from the amount of time you work. This means pushing your practice away from straight billable hours into flat fees and other compensation arrangements where you can work less time and make as much per representation.

Shave time from your estimated times of completion instead of padding time into your schedule for the work.

Rethink underlying routines of your law practice tied to set times. For example, if your standard initial consultation time is 60 minutes, seriously reconsider whether you need a full hour to accomplish what needs to be done.

Action Checklist

1. Quit padding your time estimates for completing work for clients. When you estimate time for doing work, start shaving 5% off the estimate and base your work schedule on this compressed time. Incrementally adjust estimates downward until you've squeezed the time spent on trivia out of your practice.

2. Use a countdown timer to play beat-the-clock on each client task that you do. For example, if you've set aside 60 minutes to draft a document, set a countdown timer for 55 minutes and see if you can complete the work before the timer goes off.

3. Schedule the legal work you do with enough lead time to easily beat hard deadlines imposed by courts and other third parties.

For more time management tools, tips and book updates, be sure to check out the *Recommended Resources* section at http://TimeManagementLawyers.com.

Your Notes: _____

_____

_____

_____

_____

_____

_____

_____

_____

_____

_____

_____

_____

_____

_____

_____

_____

_____

_____

_____

Chapter Five: Delegation and Outsourcing

In your law practice, do you insist on handling almost everything yourself because you never want clients to feel they're receiving poor service?

Many attorneys could "save" half their day by creating systems for handling routine tasks. Those systems should include a combination of in-house delegation and outsourcing.

If there is non-lawyer work to do, chances are you can find someone else to do it as an independent contractor or employee for a fraction of what you bill for your time as a lawyer.

A paralegal, administrative assistant, virtual assistant, law clerk, etc. won't do things exactly the same way you would. And it might take them longer to do it.

What if the assigned task takes twice as long and the results are only 90% as good as if you had done the work?

If that 90% is good enough, from a time and money standpoint you're way ahead of the game, particularly if you spent the same time working on client matters or rainmaking for new clients.

One of the key ways to save time through delegation and outsourcing is to identify one person who is ultimately responsible for a task to be completed. The easiest way to drop the ball (miss a filing deadline, etc.) is to discuss something that needs to be done with one or more people without clearly defining who exactly is responsible for doing what and by what date and time.

For example, let's say you need a brief drafted by tomorrow at 5 p.m. You discuss this with your paralegal and associate attorney because you need some legal research done and some case citations checked for accuracy. Unless you clearly define the tasks each is going to be responsible for doing so that you can get the brief out on time, chances are some of the work isn't going to get done because one employee assumes the other is doing it.

Action Checklist

1. Identify all tasks you routinely do at your firm that do not directly involve the practice of law or client development.

2. Create written systems for competent non-lawyers to do the work you have identified. Delegate the work to employees and outsource it to independent contractors. Clearly identify who is responsible for delivering what with concrete dates and times for performance.

3. For rainmaking activities, identify those you must do yourself with current and prospective clients. Delegate or outsource the rest of these activities to others.

For more time management tools, tips and book updates, be sure to check out the *Recommended Resources* section at http://TimeManagementLawyers.com.

Your Notes: _____

_____

_____

_____

_____

_____

_____

_____

_____

_____

_____

_____

_____

_____

_____

_____

_____

_____

_____

Chapter Six: Checklists

Like templates, checklists are an important part of practicing law because they save you time. A good rule of thumb is to create a checklist for each task you anticipate doing at least once a month.

The particular type of task isn't as important so much as the fact your law practice requires repetition of the task.

Common tasks suited for creating checklists include...

- Initial consultation and new client intake tasks
- Marketing campaigns to existing clients
- Filing pleadings at a court per local rules of procedure
- Essential provisions you want to include in your contracts
- Daily administrative tasks, such as trips to the bank or post office

One of the benefits of having these checklists is that you can use them to delegate or outsource work. The employee or independent contractor has a copy of the checklist to work from and you use the same checklist to review the work to ensure it's been done right.

To save more time, periodically review and refine checklists to simplify or eliminate unnecessary steps. When in doubt, apply the 80/20 Rule to ensure that the work on the checklist is vital rather than trivial when creating the desired outcome.

Action Checklist

1. Identify and rank by importance the most important tasks that take place at least monthly in your law practice.

2. Rank these tasks in order of importance to you and create checklists for the top 20% of those tasks.

3. Delegate or outsource three of the tasks for which you have created checklists. Give a copy of the checklist to the person doing the work and use the checklist to review their work.

For more time management tools, tips and book updates, be sure to check out the *Recommended Resources* section at http://TimeManagementLawyers.com.

Your Notes: _____

_____

_____

_____

_____

_____

_____

_____

_____

_____

_____

_____

_____

_____

_____

_____

_____

_____

_____

Chapter Seven: Billing

Although it's necessary for you to make sure you're billing clients accurately, there's no reason for your billing activities to eat up unnecessary time.

If your area(s) of practice make it feasible, insist on prepayment even if the funds have to go into an IOLTA[3] account because of your state bar rules.

Why?

Because you are a lawyer. Not a bank or other lending institution.

The minute you have to chase the client after-the-fact to get paid for services rendered, you've put yourself in a position of weakness that inevitably results in time wasted playing bill collector.

Speaking of time wasted, one of the easiest ways to get a client to file a bar ethics complaint against you is to aggressively chase the deadbeat trying to get paid what you're owed. Once it is filed by the deadbeat client, you must spend additional uncompensated time responding to the ethics complaint.

---

[3] IOLTA = Interest on Lawyer Trust Account

If your practice requires you to get paid after the fact, prompt billing with a short turnaround time (e.g. 14 days net) and a quick reminder notice to the tardy client will save you boatloads of time.

Of course, this means contemporaneous time recording in billing software yourself when you do the work or via a bookkeeper who enters the billable time for you in the system on a daily basis.

When you complete a legal matter for a client, the ideal time to send an invoice for professional services rendered is the same day. Waiting until the beginning of next month to bill clients for services rendered this month is a recipe for nonpayment. It's common for small law firm attorneys to rack up six figures in receivables that will never be collected.

One of the biggest mistakes attorneys make when billing is to do so monthly and provide a 30, 60, or 90-day payment terms. Unfortunately, the gratefulness of a client for services rendered rapidly deteriorates as memories fade.

The client who was ecstatic with the results you delivered becomes critical 30 or so days out. By 90 days, the client is convinced you overcharged, the legal matter was so easy that it could have been handled without your help, or that results would have been better if you hadn't screwed up.

In situations like this, you're likely to eat the time spent on the matter, i.e. involuntary pro bono, and have to work even harder to play catch-up for the lost billable hours.

Action Checklist

1. Identify legal matters for which you can require prepayment and insist upon it from new clients (you may have to deposit the funds in an IOLTA account until services are actually rendered. See your state bar rules).

2. When you bill the client for legal services rendered, where possible, do so the same day the legal work is completed instead of waiting to bill clients all at once. Use a short due date (e.g. 14 days net)

3. Put into place a series of timely reminders to send to the client once the due date has been missed, beginning on the first day an invoice is overdue.

For more time management tools, tips and book updates, be sure to check out the *Recommended Resources* section at http://TimeManagementLawyers.com.

Your Notes: _____

_____

_____

_____

_____

_____

_____

_____

_____

_____

_____

_____

_____

_____

_____

_____

_____

_____

_____

Chapter Eight: Rainmaking

Attorneys are often too busy for rainmaking activities. This means getting bogged down in the legal practice trees so one can't see the marketing forest.

However, the practice of law is a marketing business. As an attorney, you're in the business of marketing your professional services to existing and prospective clients. You need to be constantly filling your marketing funnel with prospects because your full plate of work now can become empty within 90 days if you don't.

Hanging out a shingle and printing business cards isn't going to be enough to keep your marketing funnel full of qualified prospective clients who (1) want your services, (2) have the financial ability, and (3) are willing to pay for your professional services.

Many attorneys end up with six figures in account receivables that will never be collected because they spent too much time practicing law and not enough time marketing to qualified clients. There's very few things more frustrating than discovering after the fact that you've wasted many hours performing involuntary pro bono for a client who either can't or won't pay you.

You should choose your pro bono work. Deadbeats shouldn't choose for you after the fact. Better to spend that time with friends, family, or rendering voluntary pro bono legal services for a cause you want to.

To ensure that you're not wasting your time, evaluate all potential clients based upon the three criteria listed above. Based upon your experience, create a list of "red flags" to warn you when you've got a time-wasting deadbeat on your hands.

For example, the prospective client who insists that a proposed lawsuit is about the principle of the matter instead of the money often expects you to work for little or nothing. Similarly, the potential client who asks you how much you cost in the first two minutes of your initial conversation is looking for someone who will work below market rate.

To repeat, your best clients are those who (1) want your services, (2) have the financial ability, and (3) are willing to pay for your professional services.. Devote a significant chunk of your marketing to providing legal services to these existing clients and obtaining referrals of prospects from them consistent with your state bar rules.

Don't look at this as asking for a big favor. If a client is grateful for the legal help you've provided, they will be happy to refer you to others you can help too.

Like attracts like. This means your best existing clients probably know your best potential new clients. Warm referrals from clients will save you a ton of time because you do not have to spend hours in colder markets trying to identify the same types of prospects.

Action Checklist

1. Set aside time each day to market to existing clients and prospects that want your professional legal services and are ready, willing, and able to pay for your work.

2. Try to clone your best existing clients by using them as a source of warm referrals[4] to prospective clients who are like them.

3. Save time and money by avoiding *involuntary* pro bono for clients who can't or won't pay.

For more time management tools, tips and book updates, be sure to check out the *Recommended Resources* section at http://TimeManagementLawyers.com.

---

[4] Warm referrals, of course, are subject to ethical restrictions imposed upon solicitation of new clients.

Your Notes: _____

_____

_____

_____

_____

_____

_____

_____

_____

_____

_____

_____

_____

_____

_____

_____

_____

_____

Chapter Nine: Health

Good health is essential to saving time plus extending your lifespan.

Because of your responsibilities as a legal professional, it may seem like you carry the weight of the world on your shoulders. Let's face it…being an attorney is a high stress profession.

In addition to the burnout rate (many attorneys stop practicing law within five years of graduation), there's high rates of substance abuse as a coping mechanism.

Look at the obituary section of your state bar magazine. Chances are you will see several attorneys who died in their 30s, 40s, and 50s. In addition to "natural" causes, many killed themselves through stress or, in some cases, suicide.

Frankly, no profession is worth that. If you can't find a way to cope with the stresses of your work, it's time to reconsider how or whether you should practice law. There are no brownie points in any afterlife for working yourself into an early grave.

This is not a health book. You'll need to consult with your physician, etc. before starting any diet or exercise regime.

That being said, if you've been green-lighted for exercise, one of the most efficient ways to do it is make it the first task in your morning routine before you head to the firm or even check your email.

If you place your exercise clothes right next to the bed, this makes it easier to develop the habit of working out when you first get up in the morning.

The worst time to try to exercise is at the end of the day. Chances are you've got plenty on your plate left unfinished. When that happens, your workout gets punted to "later," i.e. never.

Some attorneys successfully work out during a lunch break. But that also requires a tremendous amount of discipline because there are frequently hectic mornings where the work overflows into the afternoon. Before you know it, that lunch workout becomes a nice idea rather than actually taking place.

On the bright side, if you plan your exercise to occur at the beginning of your morning routine, it will become a habit. And once habit kicks in, it actually becomes harder to not work out than it is to invest the time as part of your routine.

Action Checklist

1. Review the obituaries in your state bar magazine and vow to never become one of attorneys who dies prematurely because of poor health habits.

2. Work with your physician to set up an exercise regimen consistent with your current physical fitness level.

3. Make exercise the first part of your daily morning routine before you do anything related to practicing law.

For more time management tools, tips and book updates, be sure to check out the *Recommended Resources* section at http://TimeManagementLawyers.com.

Your Notes: _____

_____

_____

_____

_____

_____

_____

_____

_____

_____

_____

_____

_____

_____

_____

_____

_____

_____

Chapter Ten: Incoming Data

Every day you're flooded with demands on your time as an attorney. Whether it's in-person or by phone, email, snail mail, or text message, your time gets leeched away from what you originally planned to do during the day.

To save time, you have to stick to your game plan where feasible. You're either in control of your law practice or it is controlling you.

Just because someone wants you to change your plans to accommodate their priorities does not mean you have to do so in most cases.

Unless it is a true emergency, most new demands placed on your time can be shelved and dealt with another day. There are obvious exceptions for unexpected court hearings, dealing with an issue whose statute of limitations is about to run, and other issues that can adversely affect your client and, if not dealt with today, could lead to sanctions or a malpractice lawsuit.

Yet these exceptions are perhaps 1% of the time leeches that pop up throughout the day to demand your attention.

If the new incoming task is not an emergency, simply add it to the bottom of your to-do list. When you've completed today's tasks, you can either schedule time to work on the new tasks that came in during the day, or preferably delegate/outsource the new tasks if your time is better spent on higher value work.

Examples of high value activities you should be doing include billable work for paying clients and rainmaking. If a new task doesn't fall within either of these two categories, there's a good chance you should be delegating or outsourcing it to others for completion.

This includes both law firm-related tasks and personal chores that come in during the day.

If client Smith needs a lease reviewed, there's an excellent chance you can wait until tomorrow rather than interrupting your agenda today to deal with it.

In other words, stick to your plan for today where practicable. Otherwise, you're letting events control you rather than effectively managing your practice.

Action Checklist

1. When a new task comes in, determine whether it is an emergency.

2. If the task is an emergency, handle it today or delegate/outsource it to someone who can take of the matter for you right away.

3. If the incoming task is not a true emergency, do the work you've already scheduled for the day, and postpone action on the new item until another time. Note that the postponed item can often be delegated or outsourced too if you have higher value work to do.

For more time management tools, tips and book updates, be sure to check out the *Recommended Resources* section at http://TimeManagementLawyers.com.

Your Notes: _____

_____

_____

_____

_____

_____

_____

_____

_____

_____

_____

_____

_____

_____

_____

_____

_____

_____

_____

Chapter Eleven: Off-Peak

Hate rush hour? Tired of wasting time in crowded restaurants waiting for your lunch before heading back to the firm?

Re-arrange your schedule to practice law off-peak.

To be sure, if you're a litigator, you can't force a judge to reschedule hearings for times the courthouse isn't crowded.

However, in most areas of your law practice, you can in fact adjust your schedule so that you're not wasting time simply because everyone else is trying to do the same things you are.

Does it take twice as long to commute to and from your office at 8 a.m. and 5 p.m. as other times because of rush hour?

Why are you doing it? Unless you're being chauffeured and work during the commute, you're leeching away valuable time simply by choosing to go in or leave the firm at the same time everyone else is commuting.

What about lunch? Many attorneys give up on it because it takes too long do deal with packed restaurants that take forever to prepare a decent meal.

Better to schedule a client meeting off-peak over coffee at 10 a.m. or a late lunch at 2 p.m. than fight the crowds at noon.

This applies to other aspects of your practice too, both for yourself and your employees. For example, no one should be forced to endure the lunch hour chaos at the bank or post office.

Action Checklist

1. Identify peak times for commuting, dining, banking, and other activities related to practicing law.

2. Re-arrange your schedule to commute and other firm-related activities for off-peak times.

3. Re-arrange your employees' activities so that they're handling tasks (e.g. post office trips) during off-peak times.

For more time management tools, tips and book updates, be sure to check out the *Recommended Resources* section at http://TimeManagementLawyers.com.

Your Notes: _____

_____

_____

_____

_____

_____

_____

_____

_____

_____

_____

_____

_____

_____

_____

_____

_____

_____

Chapter Twelve: Scheduling

Whether you're using electronic or paper scheduling for your law practice, you should block off dates and times for appointments, court appearances, continuing legal education seminars, and other important events as soon as possible, preferably when you get the information.

If you wait, you may forget an event and will end up double-booking time. This wastes time rescheduling at least one matter because of the booking conflict.

Before leaving your firm each Thursday afternoon, go over next week's calendar of scheduled events so you know what's coming up.

Why Thursday?

This gives you the chance to fix any potential conflicts on Friday rather than trying to do something about them over the weekend when courts are closed, opposing counsel can't be reached, and your clients are often unavailable.

On Friday afternoon before leaving the office, fill in the blank areas on next week's schedule with work prioritized according to the 80/20 Rule.

Here are two alternative ways for freeing up time using efficient prioritized scheduling techniques. Which type works best for you will depend both upon your personality and the type of law practice that you have.

First, you can use the clock-driven Time Blocking Method. You assign each day's tasks a firm time on your calendar (e.g. 9:00 a.m. to 9:30 a.m. – review Johnson contract revisions), starting with the most important item and ending with the least important item.

Second, you can use the alternative Task Priority Method. With this method, you rank each task by order of importance. However, instead of time-blocking, you start with the most important task first, complete it, and then move on to the second-ranked task.

One way to schedule using the Task Priority Method is to break up your list into morning and afternoon tasks. Let's say you have 6 client tasks you want to complete next Tuesday in addition to pre-scheduled client meetings, court appearances, etc.

With Task Priority Method, you would block off your available time on Monday morning for handling the top 2-3 tasks and then block off time in the afternoon for the remaining 3-4 tasks with lesser priority. If you don't complete a task in the morning, you can always shift it to top priority in the afternoon.

Be realistic when selecting the number of tasks you plan to do during a day. Start with 6 prioritized daily tasks and adjust the number according to your performance after a week.

The clock-driven Time Blocking Method seems to work for litigators. Conversely, transactional attorneys may find the Task Priority Method to be easier to use. However, don't discount your personality from the equation. Use what works for you.

Action Checklist

1. Schedule events on your calendar as soon as possible, preferably when you get the date, time, and location for a meeting, court appearance, continuing legal education (CLE) seminar, etc.

2. On Thursday afternoons, review your next week's calendar to see what commitments you've already made. Resolve any conflicts on Friday so you're not dealing with them over the weekend.

3. On Friday afternoons, use either the clock-driven Time Blocking Method or the Task Priority Method to fill in the available blanks on your calendar for next week.

For more time management tools, tips and book updates, be sure to check out the *Recommended Resources* section at http://TimeManagementLawyers.com.

Your Notes: _____

_____

_____

_____

_____

_____

_____

_____

_____

_____

_____

_____

_____

_____

_____

_____

_____

Time Management For Lawyers

Chapter Thirteen: Meetings

How you feel about meetings depends in large part upon whether you're an introvert or an extrovert.

In general, if client meetings and social functions fill you with energy as you interact with many people, you're probably an extrovert.

On the other hand, if spending time with groups of people and attending social functions exhausts you, and you need some downtime by yourself to recharge, you're likely an introvert.

Although this may sound like heresy if you're an extrovert, most meetings related to your law practice must be shunned like leprosy in order to free up your time. And those meetings that are mandatory (few are), should be limited in time.

Extroversion should not become a time-sucking excuse for unproductive law firm activities. If you are an extrovert, get your energy by spending your free time with family and friends, and by attending other social events unrelated to work.

To be sure, there are some meetings where you have no control over the amount of time involved. If a judge wants to meet counsel in chambers, you're there as long as the judge wants you to be there.

However, the majority of the meetings that will take place as part of your law practice are within your control even if you haven't called them.

Before calling a meeting, determine whether it is truly necessary. Would a phone call, email, or letter be as effective but take less time?

Be sure to block time for the meeting and keep to it unless a true emergency prolongs the meeting beyond the allotted time.

Err on the side of less time for a meeting. Contrary to general expectations, there is no requirement that a meeting be blocked off in 30 or 60-minute increments. If you can do what needs to be done in 20 minutes, schedule for that amount of time and no more.

One of the easiest ways to reduce time in meetings is to have a written agenda provided to the attendees prior to the meeting…and you stick with the agenda rather than going off onto ancillary matters.

If it is a staff meeting at your firm that's really necessary, meals, drinks, and snacks simply waste time. Better to have a 15-minute meeting followed by a 15-minute lunch than a 45-minute meeting where attendees are eating instead of getting down to business.

To improve focus, all phones should be banned from the meeting as a time-wasting distraction. You will also save time if you can hold the meeting in a spot where attendees can't access the Internet to surf the Web or check email.

And to speed things up, consider banning all chairs except for those attendees who have a physical condition that prevents them from standing during the meeting.

Before attending a meeting called by someone else, decide whether your presence is really necessary. And if someone has to attend on behalf of your firm, can you send an associate attorney, paralegal, or law clerk in your place?

What about meetings with prospective clients? Where possible, you should not be meeting with prospects without prepayment for your time. In addition to compensating you for time spent in consultation, prepayment puts some "skin in the game," which weeds out freebie-seeking tire kickers who want to leech advice off of you without paying for it (involuntary pro bono).

In some types of practices (e.g. contingency fee personal injury), requiring prepayment for a consult isn't standard practice. For these types of legal matters, you can still save time in two ways.

First, determine how much time is necessary for an initial consult and block accordingly. Just because your competitors give out a 60-minute consult for free doesn't mean you have to if it really takes only 40 minutes to do what needs to be done.

Second, identify tasks that can be delegated to a paralegal or administrative assistant following a checklist they've been trained to follow. Once you've got the prospect on board as a client, you can turn things over to your paralegal to handle administrative tasks that need to be done rather than spending your time on them.

Action Checklist

1. If someone else calls a meeting, determine whether your presence is required, if you can send someone else in your place, or whether you can simply decline to attend.

2. If you call a meeting, minimize the time blocked to what's truly necessary, use a written agenda, and ideally hold the meeting in a spot with minimal distractions using the tactics discussed in this chapter.

3. If you're an extrovert, get your energy from spending time with friends and family rather than

wasting time in unnecessary meetings as part of your law practice.

For more time management tools, tips and book updates, be sure to check out the *Recommended Resources* section at http://TimeManagementLawyers.com.

Your Notes: _____

_____

_____

_____

_____

_____

_____

_____

_____

_____

_____

_____

_____

_____

_____

_____

_____

_____

_____

Chapter Fourteen: Your Desk

Whether you're a neat freak or an organized pack rat, to get work done quickly, your desk should contain only the tools you'll need to accomplish the client matter you're working on at the moment.

Some attorneys like to pile the current day's work on their desk. However, what this does is distract you from what you're doing. Instead of drafting the legal document that Client Smith needs, you're likely to glance up at the pile, see the Client Jones' file, and your mind wanders to what needs to be done for Jones.

Have the client files you need within an arm's reach of your desk but out of sight. Whether it's in a file drawer you can reach without getting up, or a cardboard box with client files sitting on the floor where you can get to it, you want easy access to today's work but out of your view.

This enables you to focus on what's important for the client matter you're currently working on with minimal distractions.

Let's quantify the cost of these distractions in terms of time. Your typical distraction will cost you $1/10^{th}$ to $1/5^{th}$ of a billable hour before you're able to refocus on the work you were doing before the distraction.

If you only have your current client matter in front of you to work on and have eliminated 1-2 distractions this way, you should be able to save between 10% and 40% of the time it would have taken to do the exact same work with distractions.

Note that this isn't advice on how to change who you are as person. If your organizational skills involve stacks of paper where you know where everything is (but no one else does), that's okay. If you have everything organized in color-coded client files by topic, and cross-indexed by name, zip code, blood type, and astrological sign, more power to you.

The point of having just one client file on your desk at a time is to focus on the matter at hand because you will save time by minimizing the distractions that come with multiple files.

Action Checklist

1. Put all of your client files for today's work where you can reach them from your desk chair (e.g. cardboard box or file drawer) but out of your line of sight.

2. Clean off your desk except for the one client file you're choosing to work on now.

3. Once you've completed the client matter, swap files to work on the next client's matter but only keep one file on your desk at a time.

For more time management tools, tips and book updates, be sure to check out the *Recommended Resources* section at http://TimeManagementLawyers.com.

Your Notes: _____

_____

_____

_____

_____

_____

_____

_____

_____

_____

_____

_____

_____

_____

_____

_____

_____

_____

Chapter Fifteen: Your Books

Gone are the days where clients are impressed by rows of dusty bound case reporters lining your office bookshelves. You can find what you need a lot quicker using online research.

Most legal books have electronic editions that will save you space plus make it easier to search when you're looking for something.

In other words, where feasible, get electronic books and donate/sell your print editions.

For the remaining print editions, cull the herd by applying the 80/20 Rule.

In the pile you've identified as the trivial many, get rid of any book that you haven't used in the past year in your law practice. If you're unwilling to donate/sell them, box them up and hold onto them in storage for another year. If you don't retrieve a book for the year you've got it in storage, it's time to recognize how little it adds to your practice except clutter.

What about the remaining books?

For those you've identified as the vital few that you use often, organize them in order of how frequently you use them. Put them on a bookshelf by your desk within reach of your chair.

However, this order will change. As you use a book, put it in the location nearest you on the bookshelf. This makes it easy for you to find the books that are truly needed frequently.

What about the remaining trivial many -- those 80% or so of the books you've kept but haven't put into storage?

Place them on a bookshelf on the far side of your office. This location reduces distractions while working and puts your focus on the most important books near your desk when you need something.

Arrange these relatively unimportant books in a way that makes it easy for you to identify what you need (area of law, author, book title, etc.).

If you discover one of these books is being used monthly or more frequently, it's time to consider reclassifying it as one of the vital few and placing on the bookshelf next to your desk.

At least once a year, review your dead tree collection by applying the 80/20 Rule. Chances are you'll be removing more books from your collection.

Action Checklist

1. Transition to online research and electronic editions of your legal books. Either donate or sell the print editions you have replaced electronically.

2. For those print editions you have remaining because eBook alternatives are unavailable, apply the 80/20 Rule to classify your books. Donate or sell those books you use less than once a year, store any books you have qualms about discarding.

3. Place your important (vital few) books on a shelf by your desk within reach of your chair.

For more time management tools, tips and book updates, be sure to check out the *Recommended Resources* section at http://TimeManagementLawyers.com.

Your Notes: _____

_____

_____

_____

_____

_____

_____

_____

_____

_____

_____

_____

_____

_____

_____

_____

_____

_____

Chapter Sixteen: Snail Mail

As mentioned in a prior chapter, trips to the post office should be made off peak in order to save time.

Because you can pay someone much less to spend time dealing with the post office than the value of what you can bill for your legal services during the same time, this is definitely a task you should delegate to an employee.

How you handle incoming mail is important too for saving you valuable time.

The same employee you've assigned to make law firm trips to the post office can also weed through your junk mail. You can provide hard and fast rules for getting rid of junk mail. For example, you can give instructions for the employee to toss most incoming snail mail that has bulk rate postage or is addressed to "Occupant."

For bar association and other legal magazines, quickly scan the table of contents, and circle the titles of the articles you're interested in reading. Have your employee cut out those articles, staple them together, and put them in your "to read" bin. You can read one or two articles in your spare time between meetings or other high priority tasks.

As for the rest of your mail, make a decision about what to do with each, and put every piece where it belongs (client file, trash can, etc.) rather than letting it pile up. Otherwise you will waste time reading the same mail multiple times because you've forgotten the content after it went back into the pile.

Action Checklist

1. Assign an employee to handle law firm post office trips during off peak hours.

2. Delegate culling of junk mail to your employee.

3. Make sure you place each piece of mail you read in its proper place rather than putting back into a pile of read mail.

For more time management tools, tips and book updates, be sure to check out the *Recommended Resources* section at http://TimeManagementLawyers.com.

Your Notes: _____

_____

_____

_____

_____

_____

_____

_____

_____

_____

_____

_____

_____

_____

_____

_____

_____

_____

Chapter Seventeen: Time's Value

What's your time worth? Money is replaceable but your time isn't. So how do you quantify the value of the time you invest in rendering legal services?

During a recent discussion between a small group of attorneys in my practice area, it became clear that two firms had comparable size practices. The same number of attorneys, similar rates and client base, and roughly the same overhead.

Both firms are financially successful. However, the billing practices of one firm enables it to collect 3 times the amount of revenue per month as its competitor.

From a time management standpoint, this meant one firm would have to work at least 3 times as much as it already does without changing anything in order to make the same amount as the more successful competing firm.

Conversely, the competing law firm could, if firm chose to do so, free up 2/3rds of its time and still make as much as the less successful firm. Changing nothing, hour-for-hour the more successful firm makes 3 times as much for rendering the same services.

So how do you quantify the value of your time as an attorney?

A big mistake is to use the "standard" billing rate you see competing firms charge for the same services. Even if two firms charge the identical rate – whether by the hour, flat fee, or some other methodology -- you'll see a significant difference in net income based upon a variety of factors, including total hours billed, percentage of receivables collected, overhead, and waste.

The "standard" rate is a misnomer because it doesn't reflect the true value of the time invested as reflected by the net income earned.

When you compete for business using the standard rate, you become an average lawyer, almost a disposable commodity, in the eyes of your prospective clients. When you compete for business by charging less than other firms, even if you can do so profitably from a monetary standpoint, you're giving away irreplaceable time to do so because you have to work more to earn the same amount as firms that charge higher fees than you.

The sweet spot from both a profitability and time management standpoint lies on the higher end of the scale. When you charge more than the average attorney[5], you're perceived as being a better lawyer. As with most things, higher prices are equated with better quality while cheap screams poor quality.

When you charge more for your legal services, you can work fewer hours if you choose to do so, or even perform more voluntary pro bono work, because you earn more for the time invested in rendering professional legal services.

Will the market resist your raising rates? You won't know unless you test.

To be sure, there can be more resistance from existing clients. For those you want to keep, you may consider doing an incremental increase based upon a "logical" time, such as an X% increase in fees at the beginning of the new year.[6]

---

[5] Check your state bar rules and applicable law in your jurisdiction governing limits on attorney fees.

[6] The ability to modify fees based upon inflation, rising costs, and other factors is often addressed in the initial written client fee agreement.

For prospective clients, you will have greater leeway in raising your fees because there is no point of reference these clients have with regard to what you charge for your legal services. In other words, you haven't trained them to pay you less money.

When it comes to the value of your time, clients who have "skin in the game" will waste less of your time than those who don't. A client who covers costs in a contingency fee matter – whether by paying directly for it or being charged interest on a loan for costs advanced[7] – is less likely to waste your time than someone who gets everything for "free."

When there is a cost associated with leeching your time, clients will take up less of it. The attorney who charges twice as much as his competitor will spend less time handling the same legal work.

When you're at the higher end of what can be charged legally and ethically for your services, clients will be reluctant to waste your time for monetary reasons. In addition, your increased "quality" stature associated with the higher fees, also decreases time wasting because many clients will recognize you as a busy expert rather than someone with free time to spare.

---

[7] In jurisdictions where such loans and interest are permitted by law and legal ethics rules.

Action Checklist

1. Check your state bar rules and applicable laws to determine any maximum limits on what you can charge.

2. Subject to legal and ethical caps, start raising your rates incrementally with existing clients on new matters.

3. Subject to ethical and legal limitations, increase your fees charged to new clients. Test to see what the market will bear on the higher end of the scale based upon what the top lawyers charge in your practice area.

For more time management tools, tips and book updates, be sure to check out the *Recommended Resources* section at http://TimeManagementLawyers.com.

Your Notes: _____

_____

_____

_____

_____

_____

_____

_____

_____

_____

_____

_____

_____

_____

_____

_____

_____

_____

Chapter Eighteen: Multi-Tasking

Ever check your email while talking on the phone with a client? Send or receive text messages during a meeting?

What about reviewing a document draft while talking with your assistant about some unrelated client matter?

These are examples of fake multi-tasking.

In reality, your brain is switching back and forth rapidly between two tasks. However, you are not simultaneously doing both tasks. The consequences of fake multi-tasking are that you create unnecessary stress in your life, become unable to focus solely on one task, and the quality of both tasks ends up suffering as a result.

To save time and do a better job, prioritize the tasks and then focus on one of them at a time instead of trying to juggle two, three or more with fake multi-tasking.

Can you ever effectively multi-task?

Absolutely, if the tasks don't require dividing your attention between them. These are memorized physical actions that you can do without consciously thinking about it.

For example, if you're walking or jogging as part of your morning exercise, the motor functions involved are pretty much automatically controlled by your body.

You do not have to consciously think about putting one foot in front of the other, breathing, having your heart beat, etc. These are pretty much automated.

At the same time, you're engaging in this type of physical exercise, you may choose to multi-task by simultaneously doing something that involves thinking. For example, if you're walking on a treadmill, you can read a book. If you're running, you can listen to continuing legal education (CLE) audios, deposition recordings, or even learn a foreign language.

Just remember. What most lawyers refer to as multi-tasking is actually switching quickly between two or more tasks. It is not multi-tasking and it detracts from your efficiency and effectiveness as an attorney.

Action Checklist

1. Identify tasks you do in your practice that are actually fake multi-tasking actions.

2. Instead of fake multi-tasking, prioritize these tasks, focus on one at a time, and complete sequentially.

3. Identify mental tasks that you can do while exercising (walking, running, etc.) and save time by combining one mental task with your physical exercise.

For more time management tools, tips and book updates, be sure to check out the _Recommended Resources_ section at http://TimeManagementLawyers.com.

Your Notes: _____

_____

_____

_____

_____

_____

_____

_____

_____

_____

_____

_____

_____

_____

_____

_____

_____

_____

_____

Your Next Steps

As attorneys, we're often too busy to implement things that we've learned. Fortunately, using the time management steps in this book frees up time so you're able to do even more.

The first step, of course, is to take action if you haven't already done so. For your convenience, the next section includes all of the Action Checklist steps from each of the chapters in this book.

If you don't want to go through the list sequentially, read through it, identify one single action you want to take right now, and then do it.

Best wishes,

-Mike

Michael E. Young, J.D., LL.M.

Attorney & Counselor at Law

5068 W. Plano Parkway, Suite 300

Plano, Texas 75093 USA

P.S. Be sure to check out the *Recommended Resources* section at http://TimeManagementLawyers.com for productivity tools and updates to this book.

Master Action Checklist

As a handy reference, here is a recap of the Action Checklists for each of the book's chapters. In the print edition of this book, this master checklist contains space for you to take notes.

Goals

1. Identify what you want to do with the rest of your life, including when or whether you plan to retire from practicing law.

_____

_____

_____

_____

2. Write down 3 professional and 3 personal goals consistent with your life plans.

_____

_____

_____

_____

3. Review these goals before you start work each day and in the evening to determine whether your

personal and professional activities were consistent with your goals.

_____

_____

_____

_____

80/20 Rule

1. Identify the vital few clients who produce the majority of your income. Create a marketing plan for cloning them.

_____

_____

_____

_____

2. Identify the trivial many clients who suck up your time to add little to the bottom line. Create a plan for getting rid of them.

_____

_____

_____

_____

3. Make a list of tasks that you do unrelated to rainmaking or practicing law. Dump the unnecessary and delegate the rest.

_____

_____

_____

_____

Templates

1. Identify documents and email communications that you use repeatedly in your law practice.

_____

_____

_____

_____

2. Create templates and store them in a place accessible to you and others who will use them in your office. Where helpful, use text expanding software with these templates.

_____

_____

_____

_____

3. Set flat fee billing rates that fully compensate you for the value of the work done with each template instead so that you're getting paid for what you produce rather than the time it takes to produce it.

_____

_____

_____

_____

Parkinson's Law

1. Quit padding your time estimates for completing work for clients. When you estimate time for doing work, start shaving 5% off the estimate and base your schedule on this compressed time. Adjust estimates until you've squeezed the time spent on trivia out of your practice.

_____

_____

_____

_____

2. Use a countdown timer to play beat-the-clock on each client task that you do. For example, if you've set aside 60 minutes to draft a document, set a countdown timer for 55 minutes and see if you can complete the work before the timer goes off.

_____

_____

_____

_____

3. Schedule the legal work you do with enough lead time to easily beat hard deadlines imposed by courts and other third parties.

_____

_____

_____

Delegation and Outsourcing

1. Identify all tasks you routinely do at your firm that do not directly involve the practice of law or client development.

_____

_____

_____

_____

2. Create written systems for competent non-lawyers to do the work you have identified. Delegate the work to employees and outsource it to independent contractors. Clearly identify who is responsible for delivering what with concrete dates and times for performance.

_____

_____

_____

_____

3. For rainmaking activities, identify those you must do yourself with current and prospective clients. Delegate or outsource the rest of these activities to others.

_____

_____

_____

_____

Checklists

1. Identify tasks that take place at least monthly in your law practice.

_____

_____

_____

_____

2. Rank these tasks in order of importance to you and create checklists for the top 20% of those tasks.

_____

_____

_____

_____

3. Delegate or outsource three of the tasks for which you have created checklists. Give a copy of the checklist to the person doing the work and use the checklist to review their work.

_____

_____

_____

_____

Billing

1. Identify legal matters for which you can require prepayment and insist upon it from new clients (you may have to deposit the funds in an IOLTA account until services are actually rendered. See your state bar rules).

_____

_____

_____

_____

2. When you bill a client for legal services rendered, where possible, do so the same day the legal work is completed instead of waiting to bill clients all at once. Use a short due date (e.g. 14 days net)

3. Put into place a series of timely reminders to send to the client once the due date has been missed, beginning on the first day an invoice is overdue.

_____

_____

_____

_____

Rainmaking

1. Set aside time each day to market to existing clients and prospects that want your professional legal services and are ready, willing, and able to pay for your work.

_____

_____

_____

_____

2. Try to clone your best existing clients by using them as a source of warm referrals to prospective clients who are like them.

_____

_____

_____

_____

3. Save time and money by avoiding involuntary pro bono for clients who can't or won't pay.

_____

_____

_____

_____

Health

1. Review the obituaries in your state bar magazine and vow to never become one of attorneys who dies prematurely because of poor health habits.

_____

_____

_____

_____

2. Work with your physician to set up an exercise regimen consistent with your current physical fitness level.

_____

_____

_____

_____

3. Make exercise the first part of your daily morning routine before you do anything related to practicing law.

_____

_____

_____

_____

Incoming Data

1. When a new task comes in, determine whether it is an emergency.

_____

_____

_____

_____

2. If the task is an emergency, handle it today or delegate/outsource it to someone who can take of the matter for you right away.

_____

_____

_____

_____

3. If the incoming task is not a true emergency, do the work you've already scheduled for the day, and postpone action on the new item until another day. Note that the postponed item can often be delegated or outsourced too if you have higher value work to do.

_____

_____

_____

_____

Off-Peak

1. Identify peak times for commuting, dining, banking, and other activities related to practicing law.

_____

_____

_____

_____

2. Re-arrange your schedule to commute and other firm-related activities for off-peak times.

_____

_____

_____

_____

3. Re-arrange your employees' activities so that they're handling tasks (e.g. post office trips) during off-peak times.

_____

_____

_____

_____

Scheduling

1. Schedule events on your calendar as soon as possible, preferably when you get the date, time, and location for a meeting, court appearance, continuing legal education (CLE) seminar, etc.

_____

_____

_____

_____

2. On Thursday afternoons, review your next week's calendar to see what commitments you've already made. Resolve any conflicts on Friday so you're not dealing with them over the weekend.

_____

_____

_____

_____

3. On Friday afternoons, use either the clock-driven Time Blocking Method or the Task Priority Method to fill in the available blanks on your calendar for next week.

_____

_____

_____

_____

Meetings

1. If someone else calls a meeting, determine whether your presence is required, if you can send someone else in your place, or whether you can simply decline to attend.

_____

_____

_____

_____

2. If you call a meeting, minimize the time blocked to what's truly necessary, use a written agenda, and ideally hold the meeting in a spot with minimal distractions.

_____

_____

_____

_____

3. If you're an extrovert, get your energy from spending time with friends and family rather than wasting time in unnecessary meetings as part of your law practice.

_____

_____

_____

_____

Your Desk

1. Put all of your client files for today's work where you can reach them from your desk chair (e.g. cardboard box or file drawer) but out of your line of sight.

_____

_____

_____

_____

2. Clean off your desk except for the one client file you're choosing to work on now.

_____

_____

_____

_____

3. Once you've completed the client matter, swap files to work on the next client's matter but only keep one file on your desk at a time.

_____

_____

_____

_____

Your Books

1. Transition to online research and electronic editions of your legal books. Either donate or sell the print editions you have replaced electronically.

_____

_____

_____

_____

2. For those print editions you have remaining because eBook alternatives are unavailable, apply the 80/20 Rule to classify your books. Donate or sell those books you use less than once a year, store any books you have qualms about discarding.

_____

_____

_____

_____

3. Place your important (vital few) books on a shelf by your desk within reach of your chair.

_____

_____

_____

_____

Snail Mail

1. Assign an employee to handle law firm post office trips during off peak hours.

_____

_____

_____

_____

2. Delegate culling of junk mail to your employee.

_____

_____

_____

_____

3. Make sure you place each piece of mail you read in its proper place rather than putting back into a pile of read mail.

_____

_____

_____

_____

Time's Value

1. Check your state bar rules and applicable laws to determine any maximum limits on what you can charge.

_____

_____

_____

_____

2. Subject to legal and ethical caps, start raising your rates incrementally with existing clients on new matters.

_____

_____

_____

_____

3. Subject to ethical and legal limitations, increase your fees charged to new clients. Test to see what the market will bear on the higher end of the scale based upon what the top lawyers charge in your practice area.

_____

_____

_____

_____

Multi-Tasking

1. Identify tasks you do in your practice that are actually fake multi-tasking actions.

_____

_____

_____

_____

2. Instead of fake multi-tasking, prioritize these tasks, focus on one at a time, and complete sequentially.

_____

_____

_____

_____

3. Identify mental tasks that you can do while exercising (walking, running, etc.) and save time by combining one mental task with your physical exercise.

_____

_____

_____

_____

Recommended Resources

To help you implement the time-saving strategies and tactics found within this book, I have set up a special *Recommended Resources* section for you that will be updated from time to time. For free access, just go to http://TimeManagementLawyers.com.

If you have suggested additions for the next edition of this book, please email them to me at mike@timemanagementlawyers.com

Disclosures and Disclaimers

This Book is published in paperback and in Kindle (.azw) electronic file format for Amazon.com Kindle e-reader devices and software. Neither the Author nor the Publisher makes any claim to the intellectual property rights of Amazon.com, its subsidiaries, or related entities.

All trademarks and service marks are the properties of their respective owners. All references to these properties are made solely for editorial purposes. Except for marks actually owned by the Author or the Publisher, no commercial claims are made to their use, and neither the Author nor the Publisher is affiliated with such marks in any way.

Unless otherwise expressly noted, none of the individuals or business entities mentioned herein has endorsed the contents of this Book.

Limits of Liability & Disclaimers of Warranties

Because this Book is a general educational information product, it is not a substitute for professional advice on the topics discussed in it.

The materials in this Book are provided "as is" and without warranties of any kind either express or implied. The Author and the Publisher disclaim all warranties, express or implied, including, but not limited to, implied warranties of merchantability and fitness for a particular purpose. The Author and the Publisher do not warrant that defects will be corrected, or that any website or any server that makes this Book available in electronic format is free of viruses or other harmful components. The Author does not warrant or make any representations regarding the use or the results of the use of the materials in this Book in terms of their correctness, accuracy, reliability, or otherwise. Applicable law may not allow the exclusion of implied warranties, so the above exclusion may not apply to you.

Under no circumstances, including, but not limited to, negligence, shall the Author or the Publisher be liable for any special or consequential damages that result from the use of, or the inability to use this Book, even if the Author, the Publisher, or an authorized representative has been advised of the possibility of such damages.

Applicable law may not allow the limitation or exclusion of liability or incidental or consequential damages, so the above limitation or exclusion may not apply to you. In no event shall the Author or Publisher total liability to you for all damages, losses, and causes of action (whether in contract, tort, including but not limited to, negligence or otherwise) exceed the amount paid by you, if any, for this Book.

You agree to hold the Author and the Publisher of this Book, principals, agents, affiliates, and employees harmless from any and all liability for all claims for damages due to injuries, including attorney fees and costs, incurred by you or caused to third parties by you, arising out of the products, services, and activities discussed in this Book, excepting only claims for gross negligence or intentional tort.

You agree that any and all claims for gross negligence or intentional tort shall be settled solely by confidential binding arbitration in Collin County, Texas USA before one arbitrator, and that claims cannot be aggregated with those of any other party.

The arbitration shall be administered by JAMS pursuant to JAMS' Streamlined Arbitration Rules and Procedures. Judgment on the Award may be entered in any court having jurisdiction. This clause shall not preclude the Author or Publisher from seeking provisional remedies in aid of arbitration from a court of appropriate jurisdiction.

Facts and information are believed to be accurate at the time they were placed in this Book. All data provided in this Book is to be used for information purposes only. The information contained within is not intended to provide specific legal, financial, tax, physical or mental health advice, or any other advice whatsoever, for any individual or company and should not be relied upon in that regard. The services described are only offered in jurisdictions where they may be legally offered. Information provided is not all-inclusive, and is limited to information that is made available and such information should not be relied upon as all-inclusive or accurate.

For more information about this policy, please contact the Author at the e-mail address listed in the Copyright Notice at the front of this Book.

IF YOU DO NOT AGREE WITH THESE TERMS AND EXPRESS CONDITIONS, DO NOT READ THIS BOOK. YOUR USE OF THIS BOOK, PRODUCTS, SERVICES, AND ANY PARTICIPATION IN ACTIVITIES MENTIONED IN THIS BOOK, MEAN THAT YOU ARE AGREEING TO BE LEGALLY BOUND BY THESE TERMS.

Affiliate Compensation & Material Connections Disclosure

This Book may contain hyperlinks to websites and information created and maintained by other individuals and organizations. The Author and the Publisher do not control or guarantee the accuracy, completeness, relevance, or timeliness of any information or privacy policies posted on these linked websites.

You should assume that all references to products and services in this Book are made because material connections exist between the Author or Publisher and the providers of the mentioned products and services ("Provider"). You should also assume that all hyperlinks within this book are affiliate links for (a) the Author, (b) the Publisher, or (c) someone else who is an affiliate for the mentioned products and services (individually and collectively, the "Affiliate").

The Affiliate recommends products and services in this Book based in part on a good faith belief that the purchase of such products or services will help readers in general.

The Affiliate has this good faith belief because (a) the Affiliate has tried the product or service mentioned prior to recommending it or (b) the Affiliate has researched the reputation of the Provider and has made the decision to recommend the Provider's products or services based on the Provider's history of providing these or other products or services.

The representations made by the Affiliate about products and services reflect the Affiliate's honest opinion based upon the facts known to the Affiliate at the time this Book was published.

Because there is a material connection between the Affiliate and Providers of products or services mentioned in this Book, you should always assume that the Affiliate may be biased because of the Affiliate's relationship with a Provider and/or because the Affiliate has received or will receive something of value from a Provider.

Perform your own due diligence before purchasing a product or service mentioned in this Book.

The type of compensation received by the Affiliate may vary. In some instances, the Affiliate may receive complimentary products (such as a review copy), services, or money from a Provider prior to mentioning the Provider's products or services in this Book.

In addition, the Affiliate may receive a monetary commission or non-monetary compensation when you take action by clicking on a hyperlink in this Book. This includes, but is not limited to, when you purchase a product or service from a Provider after clicking on an affiliate link in this Book.

Health Disclaimers

As an express condition to reading to this Book, you understand and agree to the following terms.

This Book is a general educational health-related information product. This Book does not contain medical advice.

The Book's content is not a substitute for direct, personal, professional medical care and diagnosis. None of the exercises or treatments (including products and services) mentioned in this Book should be performed or otherwise used without clearance from your physician or health care provider.

There may be risks associated with participating in activities or using products and services mentioned in this Book for people in poor health or with pre-existing physical or mental health conditions.

Because these risks exist, you will not use such products or participate in such activities if you are in poor health or have a pre-existing mental or physical condition. If you choose to participate in these risks, you do so of your own free will and accord, knowingly and voluntarily assuming all risks associated with such activities.

Purchase Price

Although the Publisher believes the price is fair for the value that you receive, you understand and agree that the purchase price for this Book has been arbitrarily set by the Publisher. This price bears no relationship to objective standards.

Due Diligence

You are advised to do your own due diligence when it comes to making any decisions. Use caution and seek the advice of qualified professionals before acting upon the contents of this Book or any other information. You shall not consider any examples, documents, or other content in this Book or otherwise provided by the Author or Publisher to be the equivalent of professional advice.

The Author and the Publisher assume no responsibility for any losses or damages resulting from your use of any link, information, or opportunity contained in this Book or within any other information disclosed by the Author or the Publisher in any form whatsoever.

YOU SHOULD ALWAYS CONDUCT YOUR OWN INVESTIGATION (PERFORM DUE DILIGENCE) BEFORE BUYING PRODUCTS OR SERVICES FROM ANYONE OFFLINE OR VIA THE INTERNET. THIS INCLUDES PRODUCTS AND SERVICES SOLD VIA HYPERLINKS IN THIS BOOK.

Acknowledgements

I would like to thank my wife, Sara, for her time, patience, and help to make this book possible.

Special thanks to W. Peyton George, Esquire, Dr. Craig Childs, and Alysan Delaney-Childs for taking the time to review drafts of this book and provide invaluable feedback.

Full credit for the book's cover goes to Karl Warren, whose design skills never cease to amaze me.

My bio photo in this book was taken by D.C. photographer Joseph Allen (jallenimages.com). He's a true artist with a camera.

Last, but not least, this book was inspired by Lois Damiani (R.I.P.), who taught me the true value of time.

About the Author

A graduate of Southern Methodist University (J.D.) and Georgetown University (LL.M.), Internet Business Law Attorney Mike Young has a long history of helping clients protect their businesses by applying protective strategies to online marketing dating back to the mid-1990s.

Mike is the author of several books. His Website Legal Forms Generator software is used by a who's who in business and online marketing.

Mike is a sought-after strategist and speaker who has worked with some of the biggest names in online marketing, spoken to groups of business owners, and has appeared on many information webinars and teleseminars.

A devoted husband and father, Mike enjoys having the time to be actively involved in family life. He gets his exercise chasing three rambunctious Pembroke Welsh Corgi dogs.

Index

Printed in Great Britain
by Amazon.co.uk, Ltd.,
Marston Gate.